The Ojibwa

MICHELLE LOMBERG

Weigl

CALGARY

www.weigl.com

Published by Weigl Educational Publishers Limited
6325 10 Street SE
Calgary, Alberta, Canada
T2H 2Z9

Website: www.weigl.com

Library and Archives Canada Cataloguing in Publication Data

Lomberg, Michelle
    The Ojibwa / Michelle Lomberg.

(Canadian Aboriginal art and culture)
Includes index.
ISBN 978-1-55388-327-2 (bound)
ISBN 978-1-55388-328-9 (pbk.)

    1. Ojibwa Indians--Juvenile literature. I. Title. II. Series.
E99.C6L64 2007a   j971.004'97333   C2007-902190-5

Printed in the United States of America
2 3 4 5 6 7 8 9 0 11 10 09

Project Coordinator Heather Kissock   **Design** Janine Vangool   **Validator** JoAnn Douyette

Photograph credits
Every reasonable effort has been made to trace ownership and to obtain permission to reprint copyright material. The publishers would be pleased to have any errors or omissions brought to their attention so that they may be corrected in subsequent printings.

Cover (main): © Canadian Museum of Civilization (III-G-1696 a-b, S96-4893); **Cover (top right):** © Canadian Museum of Civilization (III-G-55, D2003-10466); © **Canadian Museum of Civilization:** pages 9 (III-G-196, D2003-10375), 10 top (V-F-186 a-b, D2004-25575), 10 bottom (III-G-1696 a-b, S96-4893), 11 left (III-G-55, D2003-10466), 13 (III-G-49, D2003-10369), 14 bottom (III-G-1642, D2005-11859), 20 (III-G-730 a-b, D2004-22832), 24 top (III-G-739, D2004-26501), 24 bottom (III-G-740, D2004-24072), 25 left (III-G-318, D2003-10168), 25 right (III-G-321, D2003-10164), 28 top (V-F-26, D2004-25333), 28 bottom (V-F-222, D2004-25323), and 30 (III-G-495, D2003-10543); © **Canadian Museum of Civilization, Frederick Wilkerson Waugh:** page 17 (1920, 48849); **CP Images:** pages 7 and 21; **Glenbow Archives:** pages 8 (NA-1269-20) and 22 (M-4372-3).

We acknowledge the financial support of the Government of Canada through the Book Publishing Industry Development Program (BPIDP) for our publishing activities.

Please note
All of the Internet URLs given in the book were valid at the time of publication. However, due to the dynamic nature of the Internet, some addresses may have changed, or sites may have ceased to exist since publication. While the author and publisher regret any inconvenience this may cause readers, no responsibility for any such changes can be accepted by either the author or the publisher.

CONTENTS

The People

The Ojibwa are known by four names. In Canada, they are mainly known as Ojibwa. However, when European settlers pronounced the word *Ojibwa*, they said *Chippewa*. As a result, in some areas, specifically in the United States, this group is called the Chippewa. Both Chippewa and Ojibwa mean "puckered." The Ojibwa were known for the puckered seams on their moccasins. In some parts of Canada, the Ojibwa are also known as the Saulteaux. This is because they used to live mainly in the area around Sault Ste. Marie, Ontario. The Ojibwa call themselves *Anishinaabe*, which means "first people."

In the 1600s, the Ojibwa began trading with French fur traders. They traded beaver skins for European goods, such as guns, cloth, beads, and metal. Soon, the Ojibwa **migrated** south and west. They moved closer to trading posts and areas where beavers were abundant.

Ojibwa Map

This map shows the traditional lands of the Ojibwa in Canada and the United States.

LEGEND
- ☐ Traditional Land
- ☐ Water
- —— Province/State Boundary
- --- Country Boundary
- ★ Capital City
- • Major City/Town

CANADA

Lake Winnipeg

SASKATCHEWAN MANITOBA ONTARIO

Winnipeg ★

Lake Nipigon

NORTH DAKOTA MINNESOTA Thunder Bay • Timmins •

Lake Superior

Sault Ste. Marie • Sudbury • • North Bay

WISCONSIN Lake Huron

UNITED STATES Lake Michigan Lake Ontario

MICHIGAN Lake Erie

Saint Lawrence River

N

SCALE
0   250
Kilomet

Ojibwa traditions changed in each place. The Plains Ojibwa lived in what are now the Canadian provinces of Manitoba, Saskatchewan, and northern North Dakota, in the United States. Like other **Aboriginal Peoples** living in the Plains region, these groups depended primarily on bison hunting to survive.

The Woodlands Ojibwa lived in what is now south-central Ontario, as well as the U.S. states of Michigan, Minnesota, and Wisconsin. They survived by hunting, fishing, and gathering.

The Northern Ojibwa inhabited the forests of what is now northern Ontario and Manitoba. They used the resources in these forests, such as plants and animals, to survive.

Bison was the main source of food, clothing, and tools for Aboriginal Peoples living on the plains.

Ojibwa Homes

Traditionally, the Ojibwa lived in structures called wigwams. A wigwam was shaped like a dome. The Ojibwa built wigwams from materials they found in nature. They usually used wooden poles covered with **rush mats** and birchbark.

There was a definite process to building a wigwam. First, poles were set in the ground. Then, the poles were bent and tied together to make a dome-shaped frame. Next, the frame was covered with rush mats, and birchbark sheets were laid over the mats. The birchbark sheets overlapped like shingles on a roof. This prevented rain and wind from entering the wigwam.

Birch trees are found throughout the Ojibwa's traditional territory.

Wigwams kept the Ojibwa warm and dry. A fire in the centre of the wigwam provided heat and light. Smoke from the fire escaped through a hole in the top of the wigwam. A blanket, animal hide, or piece of bark covered the door. The floors of the wigwam were covered with cedar bark, rush mats, or branches. People sat and slept on mats and furs. Some wigwams had low platforms that served as seats and beds.

Today, the Ojibwa live in houses and apartments on **reserves** and in cities and towns. They still build traditional structures for special ceremonies.

Wigwams were easy to build and take down. This made it easier to travel from place to place.

Ojibwa Communities

Traditional Ojibwa life was loosely organized. A group of families that were related to each other was called a clan. Clans were named after their **totem** animals. Catfish, Crane, Bear, and Wolf are examples of clan names. Groups of people who were related through marriage were called bands. Headmen, or chiefs, led bands of 300 to 400 people. During the summer months, bands lived together in villages. In the winter, each family hunted on its own.

In the winter, Ojibwa peoples lived in the forest. In the summer, they lived in small bands near rivers and lakeshores.

Some people, such as chiefs and **shamans**, held a high position in the community. However, most people were treated as equals. Women and men worked hard throughout the year. Women grew gardens, gathered berries, and butchered meat. They made clothes from animal hides. They also fashioned baskets and containers from bark. Men hunted and trapped big game, small animals, and birds. When necessary, the men were warriors who defended their families.

Children were an important part of traditional Ojibwa culture. A mother would carry her baby on a cradleboard for the first year of the baby's life. Children were rarely **reprimanded**. Instead of punishment, adults used jokes or stories to teach children how to behave properly.

Over time, there have been many changes to the Ojibwa way of life. In the 1800s, much of the Ojibwa's traditional hunting and gathering land was taken or bought by settlers. At that time, the Canadian government urged the Ojibwa and other Aboriginal groups to stop practising their traditional ways of life. The Ojibwa were forced to settle on reserves. Many Ojibwa left their reserves and moved to cities after World War II.

Today, many Ojibwa still practise their traditional customs. In some areas, Ojibwa continue to hunt and gather food. Some groups host **powwows** and other traditional celebrations. Ojibwa artists and craftspeople continue to create beautiful **artifacts** that celebrate their culture. Some students preserve their culture by studying the Ojibwa language at colleges and universities.

Small children were often carried on thin, rectangular boards called cradleboards.

Ojibwa Clothing

L ong ago, the Ojibwa made clothing from materials they found in their surroundings. Most pieces were made from buckskin, the **tanned** hide of a deer. Among the Ojibwa who lived around Lake Superior, the men wore leggings, moccasins, and breechcloths. Breechcloths were similar to short pants. Women wore dresses, leggings, and moccasins. In the winter, the Ojibwa wore warm fur robes and mittens. Farther south, Ojibwa women wove fibre to make shirts.

Leggings were often decorated with intricate designs.

Traditionally, women were responsible for making clothes. They began by tanning animal hides. First, they scraped the flesh and hair from the hides. Next, the women washed the hides and rubbed them with animal brains to make them soft. The hides were then smoked to give them colour. Smoking also protected the hides from moths, which would eat holes in the hides.

Fur and hide from animals were used to make moccasins and mittens.

Women used tools made of wood and bone to cut and sew the hides. Tools called awls made holes in the hides. Then, bone needles were used to pull thread through the holes. The thread was made of plant fibre or animal sinew, a tough strip of tissue that holds muscles to bones.

Today, many Ojibwa wear store-bought clothes. However, they still wear some traditional garments. Many people wear buckskin jackets. Colourfully beaded moccasins and mittens are also popular.

Today, clothing adornments use modern materials. The jingles on a Jingle dancer's clothing are often made of aluminum.

When Europeans arrived, the Ojibwa started to use different materials, such as cloth, to make blouses and shirts.

Ojibwa women added detailed decorations to the clothes they made. Plants were used to make blue, green, red, and yellow dyes. The women used these dyes to colour porcupine quills, which were added to clothing in elaborate patterns. European traders influenced the style of Ojibwa clothes. Women were able to obtain cloth, glass beads, buttons, and ribbon from the European traders. They used these items, along with traditional materials, to make clothes.

Ojibwa Food

Many Ojibwa groups ate a large variety of food. In warmer regions, Ojibwa women grew vegetables, such as beans, corn, and squash. Women and children also gathered berries. Some berries, such as blueberries and chokecherries, were dried. Others, such as cranberries, were eaten fresh. Raspberries were boiled to make a thick paste.

Ojibwa hunters and trappers provided their families with birds, fish, and meat. Meat was often roasted or boiled. Some meat was dried and mixed with fat and berries to make pemmican. Pemmican, which is similar to beef jerky, was a nutritious food that lasted a long time. Fish was an important food for the Ojibwa who lived around Lake Superior. Men caught fish with hooks, nets, and traps.

Some of the foods the Ojibwa ate were beans, corn, and squash.

Wild rice was an important food for many Ojibwa. Wild rice is the seed of a grass that grows in shallow water. The Ojibwa paddled their canoes through the grass to harvest wild rice. They used sticks or paddles to knock the rice kernels into their canoes. The rice was dried, boiled, and served with meat or fowl.

The Woodlands Ojibwa collected sap from maple trees to make sugar and syrup. They ate hard sugar as a treat. They used granulated, or coarsely ground, sugar to sweeten vegetables, fruits, rice, and fish. Water and maple sugar were also used to make a sweet drink. Water could be flavoured with other ingredients, too. Cherry twigs, wintergreen, raspberry leaves, and spruce needles were used to flavour hot and cold drinks.

The Plains Ojibwa did not have wild rice or maple sugar. Their main source of meat was bison. Bison meat was often made into pemmican.

Sap was collected from trees in bark containers.

Popped Wild Rice

Ingredients

30 to 44 millilitres of corn oil or vegetable oil

237 millilitres of uncooked wild rice

59 millilitres melted butter

30 millilitres of maple sugar or maple syrup

salt to taste

Equipment

large bowl

skillet

1. Put the oil in the skillet.

2. With an adult's help, heat the oil on a stovetop at medium heat.

3. Add the rice to the skillet in a single layer.

4. With an adult's help, swirl the pan over the heat until most of the rice has popped.

5. Put the popped rice in a bowl.

6. Add butter, maple sugar or maple syrup, and salt to the popped rice, and enjoy.

Tools, Weapons, and Defence

The Ojibwa used materials they found in their **environment** to make tools, clothing, and shelter.

Birchbark was an especially useful material for the Woodland Ojibwa. It was used to build wigwams, and women also used it to make birchbark bags and containers. Ojibwa men and women built birchbark canoes, too. These canoes were strong enough to use on fast-flowing rivers. The canoes were light enough to carry between rivers and lakes.

Tools made of other materials, such as bone and wood, were also important to the Ojibwa. Men used fishing hooks and lures made of bone or wood. Women used sharpened bones to scrape hides. They used awls and needles made of bone and wood to sew clothes.

Canoeing is still a popular activity among the Ojibwa. Some Ojibwa continue the traditi of carving their own birchbark canoes.

When reeling in fish, the Ojibwa either wound the line around their wrists or used a wooden fishing reel.

HUNTING AND TRAVEL

In the 1600s, the Ojibwa began using metal items. They used guns, knives, and kettles for hunting, preparing food, and warfare. They traded with the Europeans for these items.

Men used a variety of tools and techniques to hunt. Ojibwa hunters used blunt arrows to kill waterfowl. They caught small animals, such as rabbit, beaver, and otter, in **snares**. They used larger **rawhide** snares to catch deer. Ojibwa men would also use traps made of sapling trees to trap deer. The hunter would drive the deer through the forest, into the traps.

The Ojibwa used special weapons during times of war. Ojibwa warriors often used a club. The war club was made of wood. It had a heavy, round knob on one end. Knives and bows and arrows were also used in the fighting.

The Ojibwa wore snowshoes when hunting or travelling in winter. The snowshoe frames were made of wood. Strips of animal hide were woven around the frames.

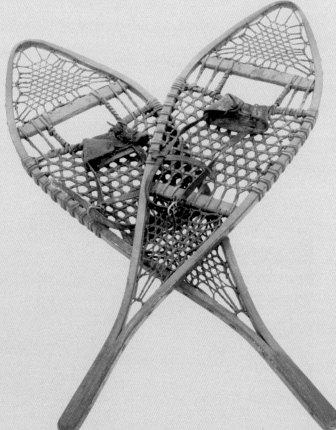

The webbing on the snowshoes kept the Ojibwa from sinking into deep snow.

Ojibwa Religion

In traditional Ojibwa religion, the world was full of spirits. The Ojibwa called these spirits *manitous*. People tried to please the spirits by praying and offering tobacco. In return, the spirits provided good weather, animals to hunt, and bountiful harvests. Some Ojibwa groups believed in a creator called *Kitchi Manitou*, or Great Spirit.

The Ojibwa who lived around Lake Superior called the lake *Kitchigami*. Kitchigami was worshipped as a giver of life. Some spirits were not kind. The Ojibwa of Lake Superior feared the *Windigo*. They believed this evil spirit was a man-eating giant. Other evil or angry spirits were believed to bring illness and famine to the Ojibwa.

In the Ojibwa language, the word *Kitchigami* means "big waters" or "many waters."

Ojibwa shamans were people who were believed to have spiritual power. They gained this power during dream quests. Shamans were usually older men. They used their power to cure diseases brought on by evil spirits.

The Midewiwin Society has been an important part of Ojibwa religion since the 1700s. It is also known as the Great Medicine Society. This society is devoted to curing illnesses and preserving traditions. Members of the Midewiwin Society are leaders or healers who receive their healing power from the Creator. Medicine men and women are called the *Mide*. The Mide invite people who appear to have healing powers to join the society. New members are taught to use plants for healing. They also learn how to conduct religious ceremonies. Members of the Mide are expected to be honest and respect other people. Other Aboriginal groups, such as the Ottawa and Potawatomi, are also members of the Midewiwin Society.

Dreams are important to the Ojibwa. They believe dreams bring them wisdom. For young Ojibwa men, a dream quest was an important part of maturing. During a dream quest, young men would journey into the forest alone. They would spend several days in the forest without food. During this time, they would have a vision of their special guardian spirit. Young women also had visions, but they were not expected to participate in a dream quest.

The Mide performed their ceremonies in and around lodges they built for this purpose.

Ceremonies and Celebrations

The Ojibwa held many ceremonies and celebrations throughout the year. Springtime brought many reasons to celebrate. After spending the long winter apart, bands reunited to build summer villages. The maple sugar harvest was another holiday time. Families worked together to collect maple sap and prepare sugar.

The First Fruits ceremony took place during the wild rice harvest in late summer. The first rice grain harvested each season was offered to the Great Spirit. The rice grain was wrapped in tobacco leaves and placed in the water where it had been gathered. Then, sweet **sage** spice was burned. The smoke from the burning sage carried a message of thanks to the Great Spirit.

The Ojibwa called the process of harvesting wild rice *manoominikewin.*

Many years ago, the Ojibwa celebrated the Feast of the Dead. This feast was held every year. The Feast of the Dead was a time to remember and honour those who had died during the past year. It was also an opportunity for people from different villages to gather together. In addition to a feast, people enjoyed dancing, games, and contests. Guests received gifts from the host village.

When they were not working in the fields, hunting, or building, the Ojibwa participated in dances, sports, and games. **Lacrosse** was one popular sport. Ojibwa men also enjoyed gambling games. They made dice from animal bones to play these games.

Ojibwa children learn about their heritage by attending powwows.

The Ojibwa continue to practise traditional celebrations. Many reserves host annual powwows. People of all ages gather at these events. They use music and games to celebrate their culture. There are competitions for dancers, drummers, and singers. Artists display arts and crafts. Powwows are joyful gatherings, but they are also **sacred** events.

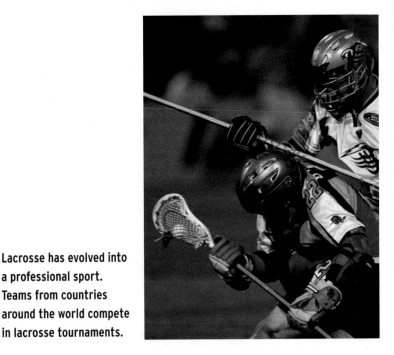

Lacrosse has evolved into a professional sport. Teams from countries around the world compete in lacrosse tournaments.

Music and Dance

Music has always been important to the Ojibwa way of life. In ancient Ojibwa culture, songs were performed on many occasions. Some songs told stories to entertain children and adults. Others helped warriors prepare for battle. Healers sang to cure illnesses. Songs were also part of religious ceremonies.

The drum has also played an important role in Ojibwa music. Drums are made from wood and animal hide. They represent honesty, life, and sharing. The round shape of the drum symbolizes the circle of life.

The Ojibwa treat their drums with great respect. The Drum Keeper is responsible for protecting the drum. He prevents people from reaching across a drum or using the drum as a table or chair.

Drums are placed in the centre of the dance area and surrounded by four or more singers. Dancers dance in a circle around the drums and the singers.

Drums are used for music and as a way to spread news. The drum will sound to announce the birth of a child, the naming of a child, marriages, and the end of a person's life.

CEREMONIAL DANCING

Dancing is another important part of Ojibwa life. Usually, Ojibwa men and women perform traditional dances separately. Rattles and drums are used to create Ojibwa music. The dancers keep time to the beat of the drum. Some dances tell stories about war or hunting.

The Grass Dance is one traditional Ojibwa dance. It is performed by Ojibwa men. The dancers wear clothes decorated with yarn or ribbon. These materials resemble long blades of grass. The dancers make graceful, swaying movements to represent grass blowing in the breeze.

Today, Ojibwa people still enjoy traditional music and dances. People gather at powwows to display their song and dance skills. They compete in singing, dancing, and drumming contests.

Ojibwa children are taught traditional dances at an early age.

Language and Storytelling

The Ojibwa call their language *Anishinaabemowin*. This language belongs to the Algonquian **language family**. The Ojibwa language shares similar features with more than 30 other Aboriginal languages. Many of these languages are no longer spoken. Schools and colleges in several Ojibwa communities keep the Ojibwa language alive. There are many **dialects** of the Ojibwa language.

Ojibwa storytellers pass on their knowledge and understanding of past generations so that Ojibwa traditions, history, language, and music can be remembered and maintained by upcoming generations.

Ojibwa	English
aanii	Hello
Aniish na?	How are you?
Migwetch	Thank you.
aki	Earth
ishkode	fire
waabooz	rabbit
mazinaatesichigan	television set
wiisini	eating
baapi	laughing
anokii	working
Nimbaap	I am laughing.
Niwiisin	I am eating.

Ojibwa families used storytelling as a form of entertainment on long winter nights. Funny stories were told to amuse young children. Other stories were about the spirit world. Ancient tales were passed down from generation to generation. Storytellers also created stories about current events.

The adventures of Nanabozho were popular subjects for stories. In the Ojibwa spirit world, Nanabozho was a hero who helped and protected people. He was also a trickster whose bad behaviour often caused many problems. In some regions, Nanabozho is known as Winabojo or Nanabush.

Members of the Midewiwin Society used birchbark scrolls to record stories and rules for ceremonies. These scrolls served as memory aids for the shamans who had to remember songs, rituals, and recipes for healing medicines. The Ojibwa writing system did not contain an alphabet. Instead, the Ojibwa used pictographs to record information. These symbolic pictures were scratched onto birchbark sheets. Pictures included human and animal figures, spirits, and various shapes and patterns.

The Ojibwa sometimes drew pictures on rocks. They used ochre to draw or paint pictographs on rocks. Other times, pictures were carved onto rocks. These pictures are called petroglyphs.

Some petroglyphs represented dreams or visions of shamans and other Ojibwa people. For example, a young person on a dream quest might receive a name in his or her dream. This special name was never spoken out loud, but it could be recorded as a petroglyph.

In the past, the Ojibwa made pictographs on rocks to tell stories and to pass on traditions.

Ojibwa Art

Art was part of everyday life for the Ojibwa. Clothing, tools, and ceremonial items were finely crafted.

Women decorated clothing, bags, baskets, and other objects with porcupine quills. Quills were plucked from a porcupine and sorted by size. The quills were dyed. Ojibwa women knew how to make bright dyes of blue, green, red, yellow, and black from local plants.

Porcupine quills were used in a variety of ways. They could be woven or braided. They could be wrapped around wooden handles and pipe stems. They could even be threaded to make jewellery and belts.

Flowers were the main theme in Ojibwa beadwork, but other patterns were also used.

The Ojibwa were also skilled weavers. Craftspeople wove strips of bark to create mats and bags. Different shades of bark created interesting patterns in the weaving.

Ojibwa men were talented wood carvers. They created bowls, spoons, and other items. These pieces were often decorated with engraved figures.

Today, the Ojibwa still practise traditional arts and crafts. Many craftspeople earn their income by selling moccasins, clothing, baskets, jewellery, and other items. These objects often become valuable collectors' items.

Birchbark biting is a unique art form that has been practised by the Ojibwa for hundreds of years. The artist selects a paper-thin piece of birchbark. The bark cannot have holes or marks. The artist carefully folds the birchbark and scratches a design onto the folded bark using his or her fingernail. Then, the artist uses his or her canine, or pointed, teeth to bite into the bark and trace the design. The tooth marks leave a delicate pattern when the bark is unfolded.

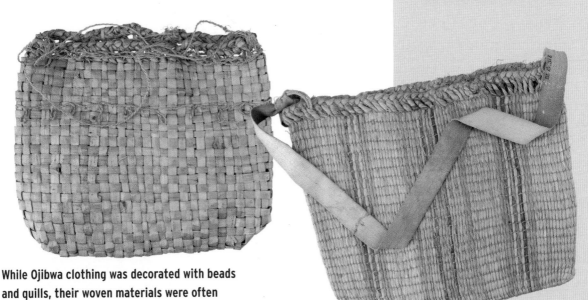

While Ojibwa clothing was decorated with beads and quills, their woven materials were often understated in design.

Ojibwa Creation

According to Ojibwa **oral** history, the world began with Mother Earth, Father Sky, Grandmother Moon, and Grandfather Sun. The Great Spirit took the four elements of earth, wind, fire, and water from Mother Earth. Using a sacred shell, the Great Spirit blew the breath of life into these elements. He created the first man, Nanabozho. The Great Spirit lowered Nanabozho to Earth.

Another story tells how the Ojibwa came to live around the Great Lakes. The story began with the Great Spirit sending a crane to make its home on Earth. As it flew toward Earth, the bird gave a loud, echoing cry. The crane circled around the Great Lakes and let out a second cry. The crane was pleased with the clear water and many fish in the lakes. It decided to live on the Great Lakes. Again, it gave a loud, echoing cry. The people of the Bear Clan, Catfish Clan, Marten Clan, and Loon Clan heard the crane's call and gathered on the shores of the Great Lakes.

The crane or heron is very important to the Ojibwa. The crane represents a position of influence. It is also a clan symbol, and members of this traditionally are speakers at meeting

MODERN ARTIST

Norval Morriseau

Norval Morriseau is an Ojibwa painter who founded a style of art called Woodland painting. Norval was born in 1932 on the Sand Point Reserve, near Beardmore, Ontario. Raised by his mother's parents, Norval learned much about the stories and spirituality of the Ojibwa from his grandfather. This spurred an interest in art at an early age.

Norval began painting when he was in his late teens. His early paintings reflected the influences of both his background and his environment. The Woodland style that Norval developed uses elements of the pictograph drawings found on the rocks around the Great Lakes to interpret Ojibwa rites, songs, and stories. This style of art has been compared to X-rays.

Norval's work was brought to the attention of an art gallery owner in Toronto, who was so impressed with what he saw that he staged Norval's first show. The show was a success and brought Norval's work to the general public.

Later in his life, Norval explored other themes in his art, including **Christianity**, spirituality, and his own life struggles. In 1978, he was named to the Order of Canada. Since then, Norval's art has been shown all over the world. In 2006, the National Gallery of Canada organized a show of his work. It was the first time that the gallery had devoted an entire show to a **First Nations** artist.

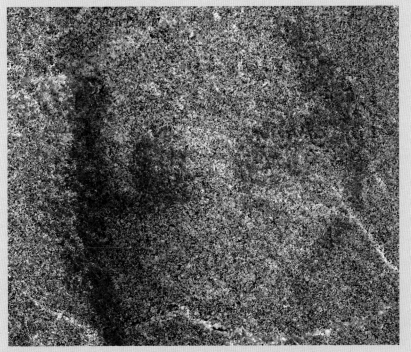

Pictographs can be found scattered on cliffs surrounding the Great Lakes. They tell stories of the relationships between humans, the spirits, and animals.

Studying the Past

Archaeologists learn about the past by studying ancient artifacts. They have learned how the Ojibwa lived long ago by studying the sites of ancient villages. Archaeologists dig up the dirt at these sites in search of tools, weapons, food remains, and other objects. These items tell archaeologists how the Ojibwa hunted and fought. They also help archaeologists understand traditional Ojibwa culture.

Oral histories are an important source of information about Ojibwa culture. These stories and legends are passed down from generation to generation. Ojibwa **elders** tell stories about traditional ways of life and past events. Elders help archaeologists understand pictographs and petroglyphs.

Recorded history also provides information about the Ojibwa's past. European explorers and traders observed Ojibwa culture. They recorded their observations. These records describe Ojibwa culture in the 1600s, when the Ojibwa first had contact with Europeans.

Skin scrapers and axes are just two types of items that have been found at archaeological digs. Discoveries such as these help archaeologists form ideas about what life was like for the Ojibwa in the past.

TIMELINE

Archaic Period
8000 BC–6000 BC

Early Aboriginal Peoples live around the Great Lakes.

Early Woodland Period
1000 BC–300 BC

Aboriginal Peoples use nets to fish in the Great Lakes.

Late Woodland Period
AD 500–1620

The Ojibwa move from the east coast to the Great Lakes region.

French Period
1620–1763

France controls the Great Lakes region. The Ojibwa meet European traders and missionaries.

British Period
1763–1814

Great Britain gains control of the Upper Great Lakes. The Ojibwa join an Ottawa warrior named Pontiac in a rebellion against the British.

Modern Period
1850–present

The Ojibwa sign a series of **treaties** with the Canadian government. Reserves are established in Manitoba, Ontario, and Saskatchewan.

Pontiac and his people had formed good trading relations with the French. Pontiac's War occurred when the British defeated the French and took over the area.

Birchbark Biting with Wax Paper

This activity allows you to try the ancient Ojibwa craft of birchbark biting without having to search for a perfect piece of birchbark.

Materials

wax paper

1. Cut a square of wax paper about 10 centimeters by 10 centimeters.

2. Fold the wax paper in half diagonally, making a triangle.

3. Fold the triangle in half along the center line, making a smaller triangle.

4. With your fingernail, scratch a design onto the wax paper triangle. Traditional Ojibwa designs included animals, birds, flowers, insects, and leaves. You can create your own design.

5. Use your canine teeth to bite into the wax paper, following along the design you traced with your fingernail. You do not have to bite right through the wax paper—just leave a mark. Make your design interesting by changing the pressure of your bites. Try varying the space between your bites.

6. Unfold the wax paper to see the design you have made.

Further Reading

Preserving the Sacred: Historical Perspectives on the Ojibwa Midewiwin by Michael Angel (University of Manitoba Press, 2002) discusses and explains the traditional spiritual belief system of the Ojibwa.

For an account of traditional Ojibwa life and history, see *The Ojibwa of Southern Ontario* by Peter S. Schmalz (University of Toronto Press, 1991).

Websites

Learn more about the Ojibwa language at **www.first-ojibwe.net/translations**.

Learn about the history of the Ojibwa at **www.turtle-island.com/ojibway.html**.

Learn more about Ojibwa communities at **www.windigo.on.ca**.

GLOSSARY

INDEX

Aboriginal Peoples: original inhabitants of a country

archaeologists: scientists who study objects from the past to learn about past civilizations

artifacts: objects made by humans

Christianity: a religion based upon the life and teachings of Jesus Christ

dialects: variations on a language that is spoken in a certain place

elders: the older and more influential members of a community

environment: the area in which something exists or lives

First Nations: members of Canada's Aboriginal community who are not Inuit or Métis

lacrosse: a sport played by throwing and catching a ball in a hand-held net

language family: a group of languages that share similar origin, grammar, and words

migrated: moved from one region to another in a large group

oral: spoken, not written

powwows: Aboriginal events that feature traditional music, dancing, and singing

rawhide: untanned animal skin that has been allowed to harden

reprimanded: severely punished

reserves: lands set apart by the federal government for a special purpose, especially for use by an Aboriginal group

rush mats: mats made from branches and bull rush

sacred: worthy of religious worship

sage: a plant with grayish-green leaves that is often used to flavour food

shamans: people believed to have special spiritual powers

snares: traps that have a rope that tightens around small animals

tanned: animal hides made into leather

totem: an animal, plant, or natural object used as a symbol by Aboriginal clans

treaties: formal agreements between groups of people